Original title:

Wrapped in Red and White

Copyright © 2024 Creative Arts Management OÜ

Author: Julian Carmichael
ISBN HARDBACK: 978-9916-90-906-5
ISBN PAPERBACK: 978-9916-90-907-2

Flickering Flames in Glistening Snow

When flames do dance and skip,
Their laughter makes the shadows flip.
Snowflakes tumble, twirl with glee,
As sparks laugh, wild and free.

A snowman claims he's quite the king,
While frostbite jokes about the sting.
Marshmallows roast with goofy grins,
In this winter, everyone wins.

Petals and Pearls in the Chill

Petals float on icy streams,
While snowflakes weave the silliest dreams.
Bouquets slip on their own charm,
Giving winter a touch of warm.

Pearls of snow, they start to roll,
Giggling softly, touching soul.
Frosty winds blow a playful tune,
While petals wink beneath the moon.

A Canvas of Cherry and Cream

A painter's brush plays tricks on time,
As cherry blossoms dance in rhyme.
Creamy clouds drift in the light,
Painting joy in snowy white.

A cherry pie, too proud to stay,
Rolls down hills in a cheeky way.
Giggling closely, the birds do scribe,
A recipe for winter's vibe.

Love's Chill in the Heart of Winter

Hearts are bold in the frosty air,
As Cupid slips on ice with flair.
Lovebirds giggle, share a snack,
While snowflakes give their laughter back.

A cozy cup, warm and snug,
Spills cocoa on a happy mug.
Winter's jest, it tickles so,
While love laughs quietly in the snow.

The Embrace of Flame and Frost

In a dance of warmth and chill,
I tripped on ice, what a thrill!
A mitten lost, in the snow,
My fingers froze, what a show!

Hot cocoa spills on my nose,
Laughter blooms, as winter blows.
The fire crackles, oh what cheer,
Yet I can't find my other shoe, dear!

Heartbeats beneath a Cherry Blossom Sky

Beneath pink clouds, we sway and spin,
Chasing petals, laughter begins.
You dodged my throw, a soft bloom flies,
And lands right on your nose—surprise!

We giggle as they stick to feet,
Each step a dance, oh what a feat!
Your sun hat's now a flower crown,
A lovely way to fall, not drown!

A Symphony of Crimson and Cloud

The leaves drop like notes from a song,
We stomp through them, laughing along.
A squirrel joins in, what a jolly prank,
As he snatches my sandwich—oh, how I bank!

I painted my face with berry juice,
Now I'm a clown, with little excuse.
We march through the park, a comical sight,
Friends and foes, all bursting with light!

Tangles of Ember and Whisper

Around the fire, we tell our tales,
My marshmallow's catching, it wails!
With giggles bright, I wave it high,
"It's not a hat, just a s'more pie!"

Crispy bits flying, oh what fun,
I ducked too late, now I'm done.
A shower of sparks, like confetti they fly,
Chased by laughter, we dream and sigh!

Twisted Ribbons of Ember and Cloud

A twirl of colors, what a sight,
The ribbons dance, with all their might.
They trip and tangle, oh what a mess,
Laughing loudly, we must confess.

Twirling round like silly fools,
Chasing dreams, bending the rules.
With every twist, we laugh and shout,
Embracing chaos, no room for doubt.

Hues of Passion and Purity

Bright colors clash, what a delight,
Mixing love and laughter, pure and bright.
A splash of joy on a rainy day,
Who knew that hues could act this way?

With hearts aglow, we paint the town,
Splashing colors, turning frowns upside down.
A canvas of giggles, oh what a ride,
In this chromatic world, we take pride.

Cloaked in Cherry and Cream

Dressed up fancy, what a scene,
Cherry and cream, like a sugary dream.
But oops! My scarf got stuck in pie,
Now who would guess, I'd rather cry?

Sweet sticky mess, laughter fills the air,
Creamy handprints, everywhere!
With every bite, we find more fun,
Cherries falling, oh we're on the run!

Shades of Love and Chill

Colors collide like hearts in glee,
Shades of love, so wild and free.
Chilled drinks spill, laughter rings out,
In this colorful chaos, we dance about.

With every shade, a joke to share,
Funky patterns, spice in the air.
Bright and bold, we own the night,
In this funny realm, all feels just right.

Dappled Light Through a Snowy Canopy

In the woods, a jolly sight,
A squirrel slips, what a delight!
Snowflakes dance like tiny sprites,
Laughing echoes through the nights.

Branches bend with frosty grins,
A snowman winks, wears my old pins.
Hot cocoa spills, a funny scene,
I start to laugh—oh! Not my jeans!

A Journey Through the Crimson Woods

With cheeky birds on branches high,
They chuckle at me as I try.
I trip on roots, land in the leaves,
In this circus of autumn eves.

Pumpkins grin with toothy flair,
I wink back—do they even care?
The path is a slippery spree,
I haven't laughed this hard—oh me!

The Beauty of Flushed Winter Evenings

The sunset blushes, a cheeky tease,
While I shiver and hug my knees.
Mittens mismatched, oh what a sight,
Chasing shadows in fading light.

Caroling tunes float in the air,
Out-of-tune notes, we're quite the pair.
Laughter bubbles, snowballs fly,
With silly grins, we live to try!

Crimson Hues in the Winter Gaze

Frosty windows, a view so grand,
I can't quite feel my frozen hand.
The cat rolls over, looking dapper,
As snowflakes plot their fabulous caper.

Candles flicker, shadows jive,
With every laugh, we come alive.
Donning hats that sit askew,
In vibrant hues, how do we do?

Dusk Enveloped in Ruby Dreams

As twilight dons its berry attire,
The sky bursts forth with laughter and fire.
Squirrels dance in coats of crimson delight,
While snowflakes giggle, a whimsical sight.

Stars wear hats, a shimmering spread,
In the chill of evening, laughter is fed.
With cheeks like cherries and breath like mist,
Winter's charm can't be dismissed.

A Romance of Winter's Palette

Two snowmen share a secretive glance,
In this frosty wonderland, they twirl and dance.
Carrot-nosed smiles in the frosty air,
While penguins waddle without any care.

With scarves that tangle and hats that sway,
They laugh off each other's whimsical play.
Frost bites gently, a lover's tease,
In this frosty ball, we're all at ease.

The Essence of Winter's Radiant Glow

Fires crackle with a mischievous cheer,
Marshmallows toast while friends gather near.
Laughter echoes on every snowy street,
As winter's essence wears a goofball's beat.

Icicles sometimes dangle in jest,
A chill arrives, but it's all in good fest.
With mugs of cocoa, our hearts feel light,
As mittens muddle in a playful fight.

Magic Wrapped in Berry Embraces

Cranberries tumble from festive delight,
While elves spin tales in the cozy twilight.
With giggles and snowballs, they play tag,
In a world where giggles are never a drag.

Sleds fly down hills with reckless glee,
While pets in sweaters are quite the sight to see.
Each snowflake spirals, a comical show,
In the magic embrace of this frosty glow.

The Ethereal Dance of Cherry Ice

In a swirl of frost they twirl,
Cherry spirits give a whirl.
Scoops of laughter, sweet delight,
Mischievous dreams take to flight.

A cone of giggles in the sun,
Chasing each other, oh what fun!
Sprinkling joy like confetti bright,
On this delicious, frosty night.

Together they bounce, so spry and bold,
Their frosty tales, a joy to behold.
With every giggle, a cherry cheer,
An ice cream kingdom, oh so near!

Beneath the stars with sprinkles galore,
These jolly treats we can't ignore.
Frosted love in every bite,
A dance of flavor, pure delight.

Embracing the Warmth of Snowy Blossoms

A frosty hug from clouds above,
Big smiles shared, a winter love.
Socks and shoes both tossed away,
Snowy blooms in bright display.

With every flake a joyful cheer,
Children shout, the fun is here!
Snowballs fly like sugar spritz,
Giggles peep from winter's blitz.

Scarves swirling in playful twirls,
Laughter dances, blissful whirls.
Frosty noses, cheeks all bright,
Friendships blossom in pure white light.

Let's build a snowman, tall and proud,
A silly hat, it cheers the crowd.
Embrace the chill, let worries stray,
Warmth of fun, come what may.

Petals Adrift in a Frosted Sky

Whimsical petals floating down,
Bouncing off the frost-kissed town.
Laughter echoes, sweet and clear,
As winter's charm draws us near.

In the plaza, snowflakes race,
Giggles painting every face.
Chasing after petal dreams,
In a land of frosty schemes.

With shivery drapes of cherry hues,
Whirlwinds spin, a playful muse.
Dancing dreams in a frosty breeze,
Nature's laughter, meant to please.

As snowflakes fade and flowers bloom,
Here's to fun, forever in the room.
Together we twirl, beneath the sky,
With petals drifting, oh so high.

Emotions on Frosted Petals

Sprinkles on my winter cake,
Frosty laughter, make no mistake.
The snowman grins, a silly show,
Dancing in a winter glow.

Giggles rise with every flake,
Snowball fights, make no heartache.
Sledding down the frosty hill,
Joyful screams, our hearts to thrill.

Snowflakes fall, a silly race,
Fingers numb, red rosy face.
Slipping, sliding, oh what fun,
Chasing joy till day is done.

The Secrets Beneath the Scarlet Line

Beneath the surface, colors blend,
Jokes and giggles never end.
A hidden stash of candy canes,
Laughter echoes through our veins.

Pine trees grumble in the breeze,
Whispers float like falling leaves.
Carrot noses, eyes of coal,
Mischief brews, it's out of control.

Underneath, the secrets grow,
Jokes shared only by the snow.
What lurks in the crunchy layer?
A tiny ghost, or just a player?

Lanterns in the Snowy Twilight

Lanterns twinkle, lights so bright,
Flickering smiles, a funny sight.
Frosty air with whispers low,
Comedic chaos starts to glow.

As shadows dance like playful sprites,
Snowflakes swirl in giggling flights.
Gloves are thrown, a mitten fight,
Laughter sparkles, pure delight.

In the chill, hot cocoa spills,
Sweetened dreams that give us thrills.
Twilight wraps us in its charm,
Every giggle holds us warm.

The Quiet Scream of Frost and Flame

Frosty lips with silent screams,
A snowball's flight, or so it seems.
Chill of winter, here we stay,
Making merry, come what may.

Fireplaces crackle, shadows play,
Soothing warmth in every way.
Frosted windows, a secret gaze,
Whispers hidden in the haze.

Snowflakes tumble, giggles rise,
As laughter sparkles in the skies.
In the quiet, let us cheer,
Funny moments drawing near.

Ribbons of Love Beneath the Frost

Balloons float high, what a sight,
In the chilly air, they dance with delight.
Scarves twirl around, laughter ignites,
Snowmen now wear colorful tights.

Mittens are lost, oh what a craze,
Chasing after them in a silly daze.
Cocoa spills down, sweet sticky treat,
As we slip and slide on frost-covered street.

Serenity in Crimson Hues

Marshmallows bounce in the bubbling pot,
We sip and we giggle, oh what a lot!
Under the mistletoe, puns take the stage,
Laughter erupts, it's the perfect page.

Sledding down hills, we tumble and roll,
Returning back home, we're missing a shoal.
Grey skies seem dull as we frolic about,
In our vibrant costumes, we dance and shout.

The Allure of Cherry Blossom Snow

Petals in laughter, they flutter and fly,
Soft whispers among the clouds in the sky.
Wearing socks that don't match is a laugh,
Pancakes are served, they're our morning half.

Sunshine peeks in, with a giggle so grand,
Bouncing like bunnies, we play in the sand.
With every snowball, there's a chuckle or two,
Our cheeks painted pink, we're silly, it's true.

Whispers of a Winter Rose

In cozy pajamas, we dance in delight,
Baking mishaps, flour takes flight.
The cat in a hat, such a sight to behold,
Chasing after ribbons, a tale to be told.

Frosty noses, with a giggle we brag,
Our holiday spirit, it just won't lag.
Fortresses built from a mountain of snow,
With laughter and joy, together we glow.

Gossamer Tones of Joy and Peace

Giddy giggles swirl around,
Like confetti on the ground.
Snowflakes dance with pure delight,
While candy canes flash so bright.

Laughter bounces off the walls,
Jolly echoes in the halls.
Mittens tangled, faces red,
Who knew winter could be so bred?

Frolicsome in frosty air,
Snowball fights lead to a dare.
Fuzzy hats and silly cheer,
Joyful songs we love to hear.

Ticklish toes in boots so wide,
Sledding down the snowy slide.
With every twist and every turn,
The warmth of friendship we all yearn.

The Silent Union of Flame and Frost

Two strange pals, they take a walk,
Fire and ice, they love to talk.
One brings warmth, the other chill,
Together they climb winter's hill.

Flames flicker, crackle, cheer,
While frost nips at your ear.
In a dance of hot and cold,
They share secrets yet untold.

Mismatched socks and toasted toes,
Bizarre pair, as everyone knows.
Yet in this freeze and fiery scene,
They prove that friends can be serene.

Cups of cocoa start to steam,
While chilly winds begin to dream.
With laughter, they embrace the night,
A funny sight, pure delight.

Portrait of a Ruby Winter

A jolly fellow dressed in fame,
With cheeks like berries, he came.
He sleds down hills with gleeful glee,
Wearing boots as big as me!

A dash of pink with ruby flair,
He brings a springtime whee to air.
With sparkly snowflakes in a bowl,
His secret recipe's pure gold.

Tickling noses, icy fun,
He races under winter sun.
With every slip and every slide,
His rosy laugh we can't abide.

A caper here, a fumble there,
Each snowy tumble raises hair.
In this portrait, we all find,
The funniest moments intertwined.

Intertwined Adventures of Bold and Soft

Fluffy clouds and daring skies,
Here come more surprises, oh my!
Bouncing around in cozy glow,
Skiing, tripping, but still we go.

With every whoop and joyful shout,
A little tumble, then we pout.
But laughter spills as we arise,
Sharing warmth beneath the skies.

Bold adventures call us forth,
With frosty air and winter's worth.
Sipping cocoa, smiles so wide,
In the joy of sledding slides.

Chasing trails, we spin and whirl,
Daring glances make us twirl.
In the light of day, we find,
Softest giggles ever kind.

Cherries on Frosted Meadows

In a field where laughter blooms,
Cherries dance like little grooms.
Frosty whispers tickle the air,
Jolly squirrels prance without a care.

Bouncing berries tease the snow,
Wiggling toes as they glow.
Mischief hides in every bite,
Giggles echo in the light.

Frosted meadows, a cake of fun,
Where playful critters dance and run.
Beneath the sun's frosty sheen,
A funny feast for all unseen.

Sweet delight in every hue,
Nature's pastry, a cherry view.
Underneath this frosty guise,
Lies a world of silly surprise.

The Conversation of Passion and Serenity

Two friends meet beside the stream,
One shouts loudly, the other's a dream.
Passion swaggers with a wink,
While Serenity just sits to think.

"Let's dance," says the fiery one,
"Why not chill?" the calm replies, fun!
They argue over music and rhyme,
While a frog croaks out of time.

Together they mix fuss and fun,
With giggles brighter than the sun.
In their antics, a sweet charade,
A blend of chaos in the shade.

Their chats, a bumpy, joyful ride,
With rivers swirling by their side.
In differences, they find their cheer,
A friendship growing, year by year.

Silk Ties of Ruby and Light

He wore a tie of vibrant hue,
While tripping over his own shoe.
Ruby threads in the daylight glow,
Make stumbling fancy, as they show.

In a world of silk and fluff,
Dapper gents can get quite tough.
One said, "Hey, check out my flair!"
The other replied, "Oh, do you care?"

Fashion battles in shades of red,
With playful banter widely spread.
Each claim theirs is the finest style,
Yet both just grinned, with silly smiles.

Laughter draped in colors bright,
They strutted on, what a delight!
With every fumble, giggles bloom,
In this fashionista's costume.

Merging of Heat and Chill

In a pot where hot meets ice,
Cooking up a wild device.
Steam curls up, wink and pout,
As chilly sprinkles dance about.

"Let's spice it up!" one chef cried,
"Cool it down!" the other replied.
They tossed in laughter, frigid cream,
While up above, a sundae gleamed.

With flavors bold, the kitchen swayed,
As steam and frost serenely played.
A spoonful of chaos in each bite,
Where every taste brings pure delight.

Heat and chill, a merry blend,
Giggles in the kitchen never end.
In this banquet, sweet meets spice,
Each bite a dance, oh so nice!

Mocha Dreams Bin the Snow

In a cup of warmth, I do float,
Every sip's a winter coat.
Marshmallows dance, oh what a sight,
As snowflakes giggle with delight.

The frothy peaks in creamy white,
Steal the chill and bring the light.
With every slurp, a goofy grin,
Who knew hot cocoa loved to spin?

Wandering snowflakes start to race,
As I dream of that tasty place.
Sipping dreams that swirl and twirl,
I laugh like a carefree little girl.

So let it snow, let laughter flow,
In this cup, my heart will glow.
Each frothy treasure, a lucky find,
In mocha dreams, I lose my mind.

Chasing Petals of Heat and Breath

Breezes swirl like unkempt hair,
Chasing petals through the air.
I tumble down in a flower patch,
With every step, a funny catch.

Sunshine sneaks in, a playful tease,
Tickling my nose like gentle bees.
The heat wraps round like a cozy hug,
While I giggle, feeling snug as a bug.

Petals dance like little clowns,
Turning my frown right upside down.
With every step, a silly dance,
Caught in the joy of this warm romance.

But watch your step, don't take a fall,
Laughter rolls like a carnival call.
Through fields of joy, we roam and glide,
Chasing warmth with laughter as our guide.

A Journey through Blushing Landscapes

On this path of blush and cheer,
I cartwheel past without a fear.
Flowers giggle as I sail,
With cheeky grins that never pale.

The trees wear jackets, bold and bright,
While squirrels jest in pure delight.
In this playful, silly spree,
Nature teases joyfully with glee.

I skip through scenes of vibrant hues,
Where every shadow wears bright shoes.
With every turn, a silly sight,
Painting landscapes in pure delight.

So let the colors dance around,
In this merry world, I've found.
With laughter flowing like a dream,
I skip along, a joyful stream.

Lullabies of Sienna and Haze

In a world of swirling dreams,
Where laughter spills like playful streams.
The skies hum sweet lullabies,
As clouds engage in comical sighs.

Sienna twirls in a lazy spin,
While the day forgets where it's been.
Haze hugs close with a giggling spin,
Letting the night's playful antics begin.

Each star winks as if to tease,
While breezes swirl with airy ease.
In twilight's grip, the tales are spun,
Tickling my heart till the day is done.

So cuddle up in this lazy haze,
Join the dance of these whimsical days.
As lullabies of laughter play,
We drift away in a funny sway.

Echoes of Fire and Frost

A snowman in a blazing hat,
Dancing with a friendly cat.
Frosty giggles, fiery grins,
Winter fun where the chill begins.

Mittens tangled in the breeze,
Chasing laughter with such ease.
Red-nosed reindeer on a spree,
Sipping cocoa by the tree.

Fireside tales of squirrels bold,
And snowy nights with candy cold.
Marshmallow dreams in a frosty bite,
Joyful chaos, what a sight!

Hot cocoa fights with fluffy mounds,
Laughter echoes all around.
Frosty jokes and frigid cheer,
This season's magic draws us near.

The Silent Song of Berry and Birch

Berry bushes dressed in cheer,
Whisper secrets for all to hear.
Birch trees giggle in the breeze,
Nature's jest, a laugh to seize.

Footprints mingle in the snow,
Who made those? We do not know!
Squirrels waltzing, what a show,
With acorn hats, they steal the glow.

Chasing shadows, frolicking bright,
Making snow angels in the night.
Sipping nectar from our cups,
As winter's magic lightly erupts.

Among the trees, we'll spin and twirl,
Red cheeks and laughter, watch them swirl.
Falling snowflakes as we sing,
In this winter, joy we bring.

Splendor in Garnet and Snow

Garnet berries, sweet delight,
Snowflakes swirling in their flight.
A chocolate kiss upon the lips,
Dancing raindrops, silly slips.

Giggling children, sleds in tow,
Racing down with hearts aglow.
Furry friends join in the fun,
Rolling 'round till the day is done.

Red cheeks glowing, noses bright,
Winter's magic, pure delight.
With every sprinkle on the ground,
Humor's charm is all around.

Warming hearts with tales so grand,
In the winter wonderland.
Cocoa spills and giggles flow,
What a splendid show we know!

Harmonies of Red and Frost

A jolly tune of winter's dance,
With fuzzy mittens, we take a chance.
Red berries bouncing in the breeze,
All around the laughing trees.

Harmony in snowflakes' drop,
Fluffy jumpers, never stop!
Twirling 'round in frosty glee,
Making memories, you and me.

Sleds collide in merry cheer,
Laughter ringing far and near.
A rosy glow upon our face,
Joyful beats in winter's embrace.

As daylight fades to starry night,
We share stories, oh what a sight!
In this wonderland of frost,
We find sweetness in the lost.

Harmonies of Blush and Ice

A penguin slipped on a patch so slick,
Flipping around like a comical trick.
The sun peeked out, a cheeky delight,
As snowmen danced in frosty ballet at night.

Their noses of carrots, quite wobbly too,
Chased each other, oh what a view!
Snowballs soared like wild confetti,
Giggles erupted, a wintry confetti.

Threads of Scarlet and Soft White

A knitter's yarn tangled in quite a mess,
While fighting off cats, what a test!
Stitches fly in a playful fight,
With every tug, laughter takes flight.

Sweaters emerge, though not quite right,
One arm is too long, a comical sight.
A scarf that's a blanket, a hat for the floor,
Fashion faux pas, we can't help but roar!

Echoes of Brightness and Silence

In a snowstorm, a brave soul dared to sing,
Echoes bouncing, oh what joy they bring!
A squirrel joined with a cheeky grunt,
Creating a chorus, a merry front.

Frosty whispers giggled and cheered,
As snowflakes flew, they cheerfully sneered.
With every slip, more laughter ensued,
Winter's great jest, we gladly pursued.

The Caress of Fire and Snow

A marshmallow fell, plopped in the frost,
Toasty and gooey, what a sweet cost!
While fire crackled, the warmth we adore,
The snowman plotted to even the score.

With frosty fingers, he reached for a treat,
To roast over flames, oh what a feat!
But in the end, he merely watched tight,
As the gooey goodness drifted out of sight.

The Charm of Rose Petal Snow

When petals drift like winter's glee,
A sneezing fit from me you see.
They whisper soft with gentle grace,
In gardens pink, I lose my place.

The sunbeams laugh upon the ground,
A ticklish tease, oh, what a sound!
I chase the blooms, they dance away,
While butterflies engage in play.

The wind brings scents both sweet and bright,
While pollen lands, oh, what a fright!
With every step, I trip and fall,
A comedy, my funny call.

So let them float, those jokes in air,
Life's bloom of laughter, full of flair.
In chaos of pink, I find my bliss,
A petal shower, not to miss!

Secrets Carried on Scarlet Winds

A tale is told by winds so sly,
With whispers bold, they soar and fly.
They dance around, a cheeky crew,
With lights ablaze in hues of hue.

Secrets float on crimson breath,
Laughter echoes, teasing death.
While hearts are ticking, mischief grins,
Oh, what delight in scarlet spins!

The leaves, they giggle as they play,
In swirling games, they drift away.
I chase the tales beneath my hat,
While squirrels plot a cheeky spat.

And here's the catch, dear friend of mine,
All these giggles, oh, how they shine!
In fluttered paths of windy bliss,
A secret dance—a playful kiss!

A Melancholic Dance of Red Dawn

As morning breaks, a curtain drawn,
In vibrant hues, the world is born.
With sleepy eyes, I sigh and yawn,
A fumble here—oh, what a con!

The coffee spills, it stains my socks,
A dance of clumsy morning clocks.
With shades of tangerine and blush,
I pirouette in sleepy hush.

My slippers squeak, they have a say,
A duet played in disarray.
While toast jumps high, a crunchy burst,
I laugh aloud, it's morning's thirst!

Though dawn may cry in colors bold,
A humorous tale of dreams retold.
Each moment shared, a warm embrace,
In landscapes ripe with funny grace!

Glimpses of Winter in Burgundy

The winter winks in berry tone,
While frosty winds throw ice and bone.
I bundle up in layers tight,
With mismatched gloves—a laugh, no fright!

The snowflakes tease, they swirl and swirl,
A frosty dance, a winter whirl.
I trip and tumble in a mound,
A giggle echoes all around.

While mugs of cocoa warm the heart,
A dash of cream, they're quite the art.
In sips and slurps, we raise a cheer,
As laughter warms the chilly sphere.

So raise a toast to winter's fun,
In burgundy hues, our day's begun.
With friends and glee, we frolic free,
In the snowy charm of jubilee!

Crimson Threads and Frosted Dreams

In a jolly season bright,
Knitted mittens take their flight,
Snowflakes giggle, dance and twirl,
While scarves spin in a merry whirl.

Balloons in shades of berry burst,
Laughter flows, it's just the first,
Mittens mishaps, oh what a sight,
Friends diving in a snowball fight!

A nose so red, a joke anew,
Sipping cocoa, it's all askew,
The quilted couch, a cozy bed,
Amidst the warmth, we laugh instead.

With crimson joys and frosted cheer,
We'll dance beneath the atmosphere,
Piecing together threads of fun,
In this playful, snowy run.

Whispering Colors of the Heart

Colorful whispers in the air,
Tickling toes without a care,
Painting smiles on snowy cheeks,
With every giggle, laughter peaks.

Kites pulled tight on bracing winds,
Chasing clouds, let fun begin,
Red-nosed pranks around the bend,
A snowflake-fight that won't quite end.

Socks mismatched, what a delight,
Jumping high with sheer delight,
Winter glow and merry play,
A canvas bright, we paint the day!

Whispers shared 'neath frosty skies,
With friends aplenty and merry sighs,
Colors blending, hearts aglow,
In the joy of winter's show.

The Dance of Scarlet and Ivory

Scarlet dresses swirl and spin,
While ivory snowflakes brush the skin,
Laughter echoes, a playful sound,
As twirls ignite the snowy ground.

A tumble here, a slip over there,
Mismatched mittens filled with flair,
Chasing friends in a snowy maze,
We giggle, blush, in winter's gaze.

Sleds zoom by with squeals of glee,
Dancing snowflakes call to me,
With splashes of red and hints of cream,
Winter's dream is but a theme.

So we laugh and dance with zest,
In this frosted winter fest,
Together we'll embrace the chill,
In winsome joy, we keep the thrill.

Veils of Ruby and Snow

Veils of rubies flutter bright,
In snowy fields, a whimsical sight,
Laughter trails like softest snow,
As puppies race and friends all glow.

Red hats bobbing up and down,
In the merry, snowy town,
Frosty cheeks and chitter chatter,
Each joke shared, the laughter's batter.

Snowmen grinning wide and tall,
With carrot noses daring to sprawl,
A playful nudge, a frosty fling,
In this charmed winter swing.

So we drape in blankets warm,
While outside swirls a cozy storm,
With ruby hues and snowy threads,
Creating giggles in our beds.

Sipped Warmth in Berry Breaths

In a cup of cheer, so sweet and bright,
A splash of joy, a dash of delight.
Laughter bubbles, like soda pop,
With every sip, we just can't stop.

Strawberries giggle, in frothy foam,
While we dance around in our cozy home.
Cherries sing songs of the silly and spry,
As we savor the warmth, letting worries fly.

A banana slips, right on the floor,
With a comical tumble, we all want more!
Sippin' our treats with goofy grins wide,
Berry breaths hugging us, joy can't hide.

So raise your mugs to this quirky cheer,
With warmth in each gulp, let's toast to the year!
As berry delights mix with laughter and fun,
In this fizzy wonder, our hearts come undone.

Snowflakes Resting on Ruby Lips

Frosty kisses fall soft and light,
On cheeks so red, a comical sight.
Snowflakes make friends on our mugs warm,
They giggle together, that's their charm!

Chubby snowmen roll in playful cheer,
While ruby lips whisper, "Can I have a beer?"
A snowball fight erupts, oh what a show,
With laughter like bells in the blankets of snow.

Sledding down hills, making big flops,
Landing in snowdrifts with playful pops.
The cold bites gently, but we don't mind,
With ruby lips shining, our hearts intertwined.

So let's toast to winter, with joy and with lips,
Painting the town with our frosty quips.
As snowflakes gather, with stories to spill,
We'll laugh and enjoy, winter's quirky thrill.

A Portrait of Winter's Heart

Snowmen pose for a silly display,
With carrot noses, they steal the day.
Frosty friends with the warmest of grins,
In a world painted white, the giggling begins.

Icicles dangle like comical teeth,
Hanging from gutters with frosty wreaths.
With every chill in the playful air,
Comes laughter and joy that we all want to share.

A holiday feast with pies that wobble,
While uncle Joe tells tales of his bobble.
Around the table, in laughter we drown,
With goofy grins spread all around town.

So here's to winter, in all its quirky charm,
With coats bundled up, safe from harm.
In portraits of fun, we hold dear,
Winter's heart beats lively, let's give a cheer!

Whispered Promises in Cherry Blossoms

In springtime's blush, there's giggles galore,
As blossoms take flight and our spirits soar.
Cherry trees dance, in a whimsical tune,
While bees waddle by, wearing hats of buffoon.

Petals flutter down like whispers of cheer,
Tickling our noses, drawing friends near.
With promises sweet, like candy to taste,
We twirl in delight, not a moment to waste.

Silly secrets shared in the dappled light,
As blossoms erupt, a remarkable sight.
Cherry laughs echo through parks and around,
With joy blooming bright, is sweet laughter found?

So let's celebrate spring with a twist and a joke,
In the soft gentle breeze, let our spirits provoke.
As whispered promises bloom and delight,
In a sea of cherry fun, hearts feel so light!

The Embrace of Scarlet Shadows

In a coat of crimson flair,
I tripped on bright balloon air.
Snowmen grinned with carrot dreams,
While I plotted silly schemes.

Laughter danced beneath the trees,
Frolicking with the chilly breeze.
My scarf flew like a dapper kite,
As I tumbled into pure delight.

Every snowflake had its say,
Twirling jokes in a gleeful display.
With each laugh, the cold grew warm,
In this kaleidoscope of charm.

So, let us prance, let's make a mess,
In this vibrant winter dress.
With smiles bright and giggles shared,
Who knew cold could be so flared!

Frost-kissed Carnation Dreams

A blush of hue on frosty cheeks,
We skated past with silly shrieks.
Those rosy cheeks, we wore with pride,
While giggling snowflakes danced and slid.

In frozen fields of cotton fluff,
We tossed snowballs, that was tough!
But every aim became a laugh,
As we slipped into our frosty bath.

The sun peeked through, a cheeky grin,
As we bundled up, ten layers in.
But oh, the style, it couldn't hide,
Our twirling spirits in winter's tide.

So come, let's chase that fleeting light,
In this carnival of dazzling white.
With every flutter and a cheer,
Frost-kissed dreams keep drawing near!

A Symphony in Ruby and Ivory

A jingle bell rang, it hit a tree,
With a pop of joy, oh so free.
We danced like shadows in swirling bliss,
While snowflakes fluttered, hugged, and kissed.

Ruby hats piled high, like candy canes,
All around, merry laughter reigns.
Slipping and sliding with giggles loud,
In a flurry of fun, we were proud.

The sun set low, casting long fun shadows,
As we painted the night like daring gallows.
With each goofy move, our spirits soared,
In this winter wonder, we all adored.

So let's grab a cup of cocoa cheer,
And share our blunders, year after year.
With ruby glee and ivory light,
We'll dance 'til dawn, hearts feeling bright!

The Dance of Blushing Snowflakes

Underneath a moonlit hue,
We twirled in outfits, oh so askew.
Snowflakes giggled, rolled on the ground,
In this wild party, fun's profound.

Each leap we took sent giggles flying,
As snowy laughter kept on trying.
With rosy cheeks, we spun around,
Creating joy where joy is found.

The chilly air, it tickled our noses,
With every step, we struck silly poses.
Our dance of whimsy, delight every way,
In this wintry bliss, let's laugh and play.

So raise a glass of frosty cheer,
To every moment, every silly sphere.
With blushing snowflakes in every turn,
Let the fires of laughter happily burn!

The Emblem of Velvet and Frost

In a land where the snowflakes glide,
There's a creature with cheeks all bright,
He waddles around, full of cheer,
Telling jokes that tickle the night.

With mittens too big on his paws,
He slips and he slides, what a sight!
Falling then laughing, he pauses,
As snowmen cheer with delight.

His nose is a button, a classic design,
But it wiggles when he speaks, oh so funny!
With laughter that echoes, it's simply divine,
As ice cream cones melt, oh honey!

Even the squirrels chuckle and fade,
As he dances, a whimsical spree,
In this frosty realm, memories are made,
A jolly belly flop in glee!

Beauty in the Blooming Silence

In gardens where petals softly sway,
A gopher peeks out, curious and spry,
He wears a hat fashioned from hay,
As butterflies giggle and sigh.

The daisies smirk, whispering secrets,
To the roses who blush with a tune,
While rabbits perform little ballet feats,
In rhythms below the bright moon.

Bees buzz a chorus, sweet and absurd,
As they bumble and stumble through air,
With laughter that needs not a word,
Nature plays a tune with flair.

When the wind teases through little leaves,
All creatures are swaying in bliss,
It's a dance of joy where nobody grieves,
In silence where giggles, they'll miss!

The Enigma of Blush and Chill

A jolly snowman with a carrot nose,
Is ready to giggle and prance,
He plays hide and seek with frosty woes,
In a flurry of laughter, he'll dance.

With cheeks so rosy, they shine bright,
He shares tales of winter delight,
The penguins come join for a laugh,
As they shuffle and slide, what a sight!

Sometimes he trips on his floppy hat,
And tumbles with a thud, oh dear!
But with chuckles and snorts, how about that?
Hot cocoa awaits with holiday cheer!

A riddle unraveled with snowflakes near,
In chilly whispers, we find the fun,
Under the moonlight, let's all cheer,
For joy will be brightened by everyone!

A Harmonious Chill in the Air

In a town where the icicles play,
Two penguins are plotting a scheme,
With snowballs and giggles, they sway,
Planning a snowball fight, what a dream!

The children all gather, eyes aglow,
As laughter echoes through the square,
Snowmen look on, with a smile to show,
Joy swirling around in the cold air.

Each throw and slip, a grand ballet,
As the snowflakes tumble from the sky,
A humorous twirl, and then, hooray!
They find their own way to fly high!

As the sun dips low, colors ignite,
In the chill, friendships bloom and flare,
With giggles that pop on this frosty night,
Our hearts beat in tune, oh what a pair!

Milton Keynes UK
Ingram Content Group UK Ltd.
UKHW020046271124
451585UK00012B/1095

9 789916 909072